# Academic Presenting and Presentations

Teacher's Book

# Further components in this series

| | |
|---|---|
| Student's Book | ISBN 978-3-7347-8367-8 |
| Downloadable videos | www.linguabooks.com/app |
| Video DVD | info@linguabooks.com |

www.linguabooks.com

# Academic Presenting and Presentations

A preparation course for university students

LinguaBooks
The Elsie Whiteley Innovation Centre
Hopwood Lane
Halifax
West Yorkshire
HX1 5ER
United Kingdom

www.linguabooks.com

An imprint of
LinguaServe GbR
Zerrennerstr. 26
75217 Pforzheim
Germany

www.linguaserve.eu

# Contents

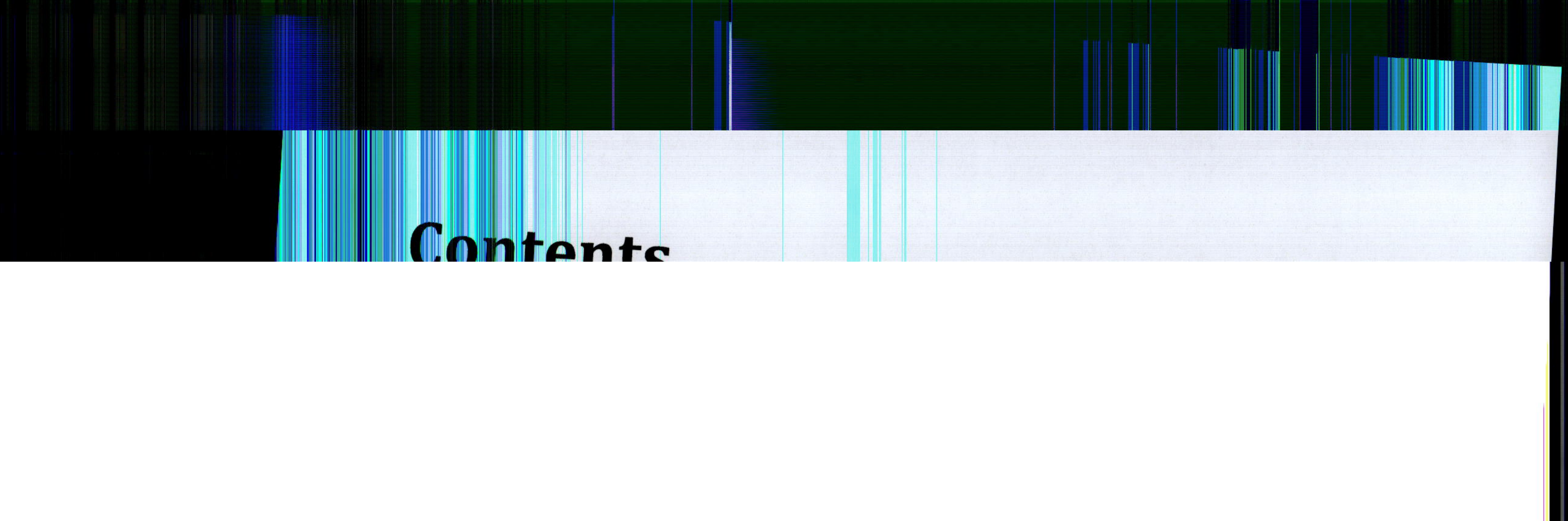

*"I hope I remember everything," said Toni.*
*"You won't," said Trapp. "That's how you learn."*


Louis Sachar, The Cardturner

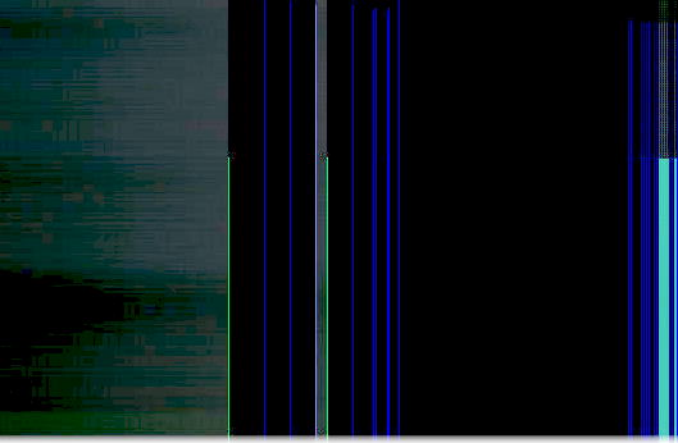

The presentations are available online and can be found on the *Academic Presenting and Presentations* website at:

http://www.linguabooks.com/app

A boxed set of Video DVDs is also available from the publishers. This contains videos of all the Sample Presentations and Learning Presentations in a format suitable for playing on a standard DVD player.

This Teacher's Book includes general guidance for class work, detailed notes on each unit and details of the theoretical rationale on which the course is based.

Information in an academic presentation must be verifiable and the presenter must have a wider and deeper knowledge of the topic than that presented in the body of the presentation. A presentation should lead to discussion and further debate, with the presenter able to respond to audience questions competently. Different genres of academic presentation (e.g. presenting a paper, research presentations or problem-solution presentations) will require students to employ an appropriate structure.

**A presentation-driven course**

*Academic Presenting and Presentations* is built around presentations. This is based on the belief that the more presentations students see, the more clearly they will develop their ideas about what makes a presentation successful and what constitutes an appropriate academic presentation. There are two types of presentation in *Academic Presenting and Presentations:* **Learning Presentations** and **Sample Presentations**.

- **The Learning Presentations (LP)** give students information and advice about different aspects of presenting. While the focus of these presentations is on the advice given to students, they can also be used as examples of presentations in themselves and analysed for issues such as useful presenting language or delivery techniques.

- **The Sample Presentations (SP)** give students a chance to see different types of presentation in action and therefore become familiar with different genres of academic presentation. The emphasis while watching these presentations is on seeing how different presentations work structurally and how a presentation can be delivered successfully. A review of these presentations is provided in each unit of the Student's Book and useful language is highlighted there. If you are not familiar

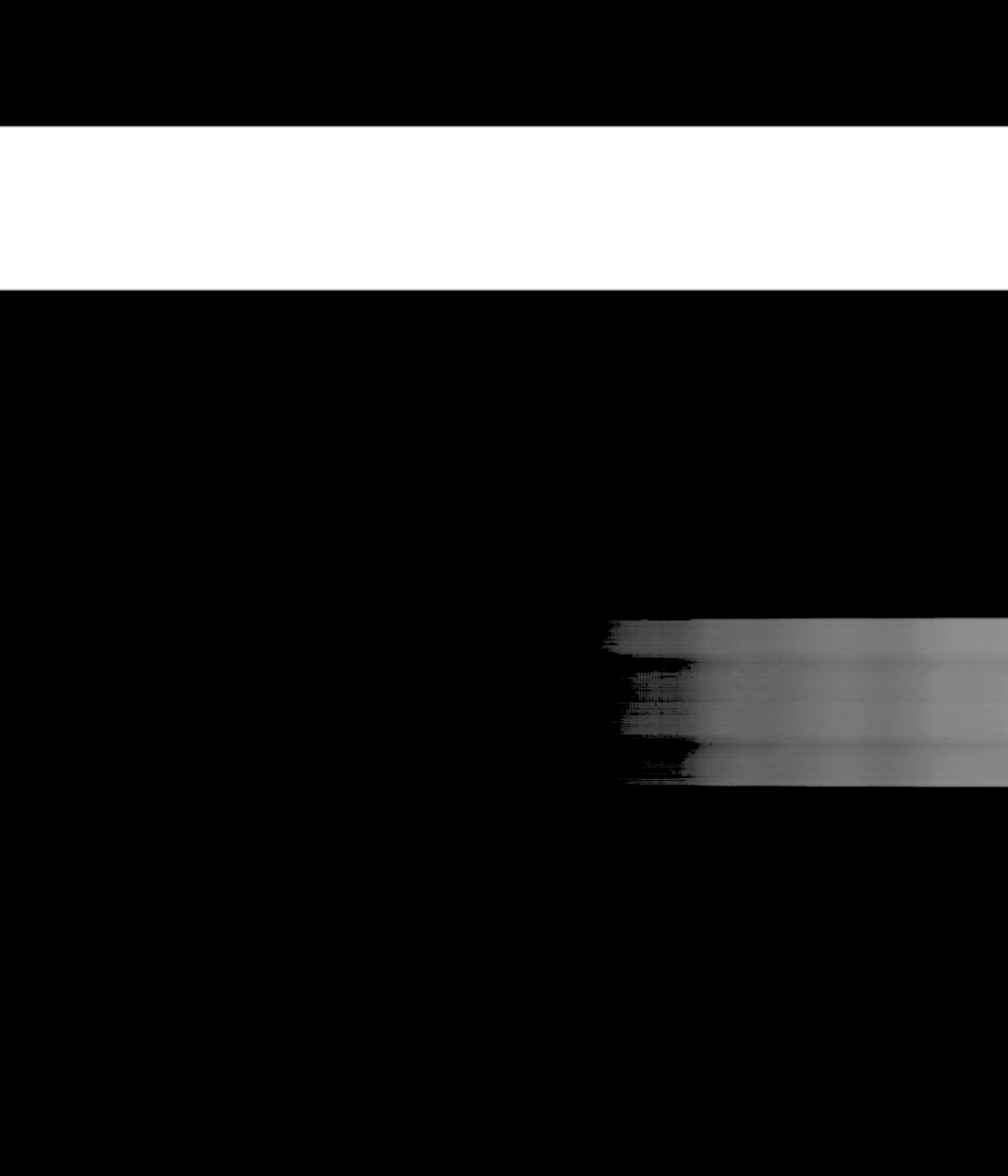

- **Genre analysis:** In the same way that students may be expected to incorporate certain step during different types of essay, they should be using similar steps in different types of presentation. This means *Academic Presenting and Presentations* goes deeper into the structure of a presentation than simply introduction-body-conclusion. Students are encouraged to structure their presentations according to the objective of their presentation and their audience.

## Class management

A presentation classroom should be lively. Encourage students to see the preparation process of a presentation as an active process. Rather than silent scripting or rehearsal, encourage students to prepare and practice as if giving the presentation. In this way, they can think about what they want to say, how they want to deliver it and what gestures to use.

For this reason, the Student's Book does not give any specific guidance on class management, e.g. whether to work in pairs or in groups. This is because the organisation of your group will depend on the logistics. The aim should be to give each student as many opportunities present as possible, either to small groups or to the whole class. Teachers should also be aware of the distracting impact of simultaneous presentations taking place in different parts of the room.

Since rehearsal is a vital step in the presentation process, consider using a carousel system along the lines of speed dating. Have some students sitting around the room whilst other students move from one person or group to the next, delivering a part of their presentation and then moving on. This type of practice could be particularly beneficial for more reticent students, providing them with multiple opportunities to practice the delivery of their presentation in a relatively stress-free way. There should also be opportunities for students

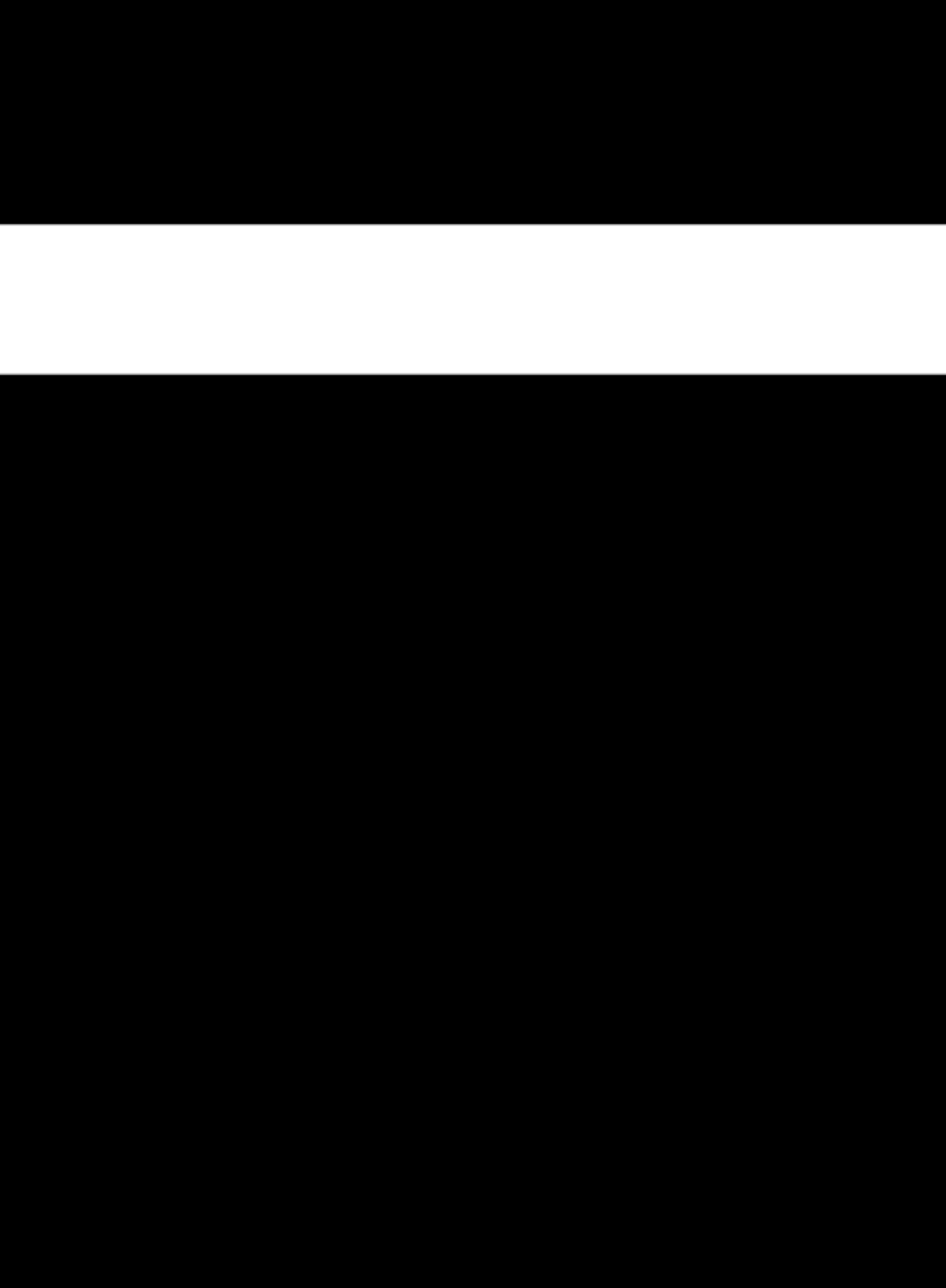

At the end of the unit, these questions could be returned to for a further class discussion in order to check how much of the course the students have taken on board and to see how their ideas have developed. This will help mark the progress of the course and indicate where more work may be needed.

**Presentation tasks**

There are eleven formal presentation tasks in *Academic Presenting and Presentations*, although you may also take other opportunities (e.g. summary of a group discussion) to give students presentation practice. The earlier presentation tasks are designed to help students become comfortable presenting generally. From Presentation Task 7 onwards, the academic integrity of the presentations take on a greater significance. There must be reliable and academically suitable material in the presentations and, consequently, they will take longer to prepare. The page numbers in the following table refer to the Student's Book.

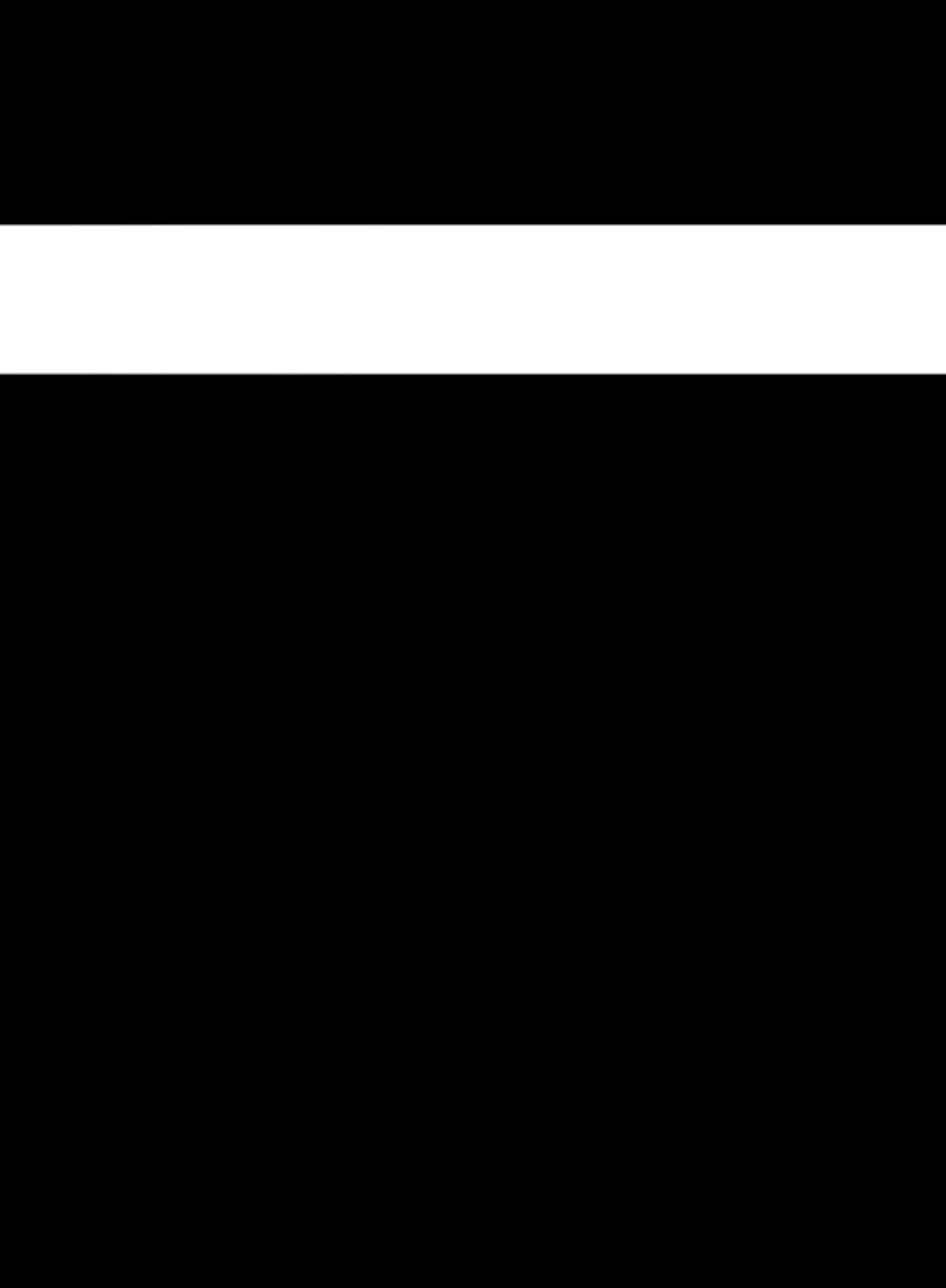

**Preparing presentations**

When students are preparing their presentations, monitor the class carefully and provide any assistance students might need with particular vocabulary items or ways of expressing their ideas. This is an opportunity to focus on things like individual learner pronunciation issues. When students are preparing, push them towards having flexibility of expression. Ask them how else they could say the same thing. Encouraging a variety of expression will help students rely less on fully scripted presentations and enable them to present more naturally. Varied repetition of different sections of a presentation can be very useful in terms of developing a more natural presentation style.

Preparation can also be set as homework, but make sure there is some class time for preparation to enable you or peers to give feedback before the delivery stage. To try to help students really develop their presentation skills avoid giving too little preparation time. A poorly prepared or poorly rehearsed presentation has limited learning opportunities besides learning to prepare more thoroughly. Even a one-minute presentation is going to take time to develop, so factor this into the planning.

When students are working together in the preparation stage, push them to notice positive and poor presentation features and ask what aspects of another person's presentation style they could use to improve their own presentation skills.

During this stage, also consider how students are using scripts/notes. A general contention of *Academic Presenting and Presentations* is that full scripting should be avoided. Early in a presentation course, however, students might want the security of a script. Encourage them towards the use of note cards and bullet points. A note-card template is provided as one of the photocopiable worksheets at the back of the Student's Book. If students are using note-cards,

**Presentation questions**

The question and answer part of a presentation is highly valued by lecturers as it is this part of the presentation where a true measurement of a student's understanding can be taken. It is also expected that a successful academic presentation will initiate wider discussion. Although strategies for dealing with questions are not covered until Unit 6, students should be asking questions after presentations throughout the course and should be encouraged to identify when someone deals with questions well or fails to do so.

**Presentation feedback**

Although this is a presentation skills course, it is an *academic* presentation skills course. This means presentations have to be considered on a deeper level than technical presentation expertise alone. Content matters. When giving feedback, ensure students consider issues like strength of argument, overall success of presentation in meeting its aim, use of support and evidence. As well as tutor feedback, peer feedback should also be strongly encouraged.

It can be very valuable to see presentation style as a member of the audience through the use of video. Once students have become more comfortable presenting, you could consider videoing their presentations. This could be potentially stressful, so only do it with student consent and, initially, avoid whole group feedback or showing the video to the whole group. The student could watch their presentation and provide their own feedback to you regarding its strengths and areas which could be improved. Video can also be very motivating if students are able to see how their presentation skills develop, either through repeated practice of the same presentation or over the full *Academic Presenting and Presentations* course.

You can also provide opportunities for students to deliver their presentations again on the basis of the initial feedback.

# Learning Presentations

| Unit | Presentation Title |
|:---:|:---|
| 1 | **1.1 – Introduction To Presentations** – The Basics |
| | **1.2 – What Makes A Good Presentation** – Making Sure Your Presentation Has A POINT |
| | **1.3 – Presentation Task** – Presentations and Me |
| 2 | **2.1 – The Academic Presentation** – Key Features of Academic Presentations |
| | **2.2 – Presentation As Performance** – Developing Your Presentation Voice |
| 3 | **3.1 – Presenting A Paper** – Make Your Opinion Known |
| | **3.2 – Presenting More Than One Paper** – Horizontal vs. Vertical |
| 4 | **4.1 – Group Presentations** – Everyone Has A Role |
| | **4.2 – Designing A Poster** – Making An Impact |
| | **4.3 – Elevator Pitch Presentations** – Making A Point in 30 Seconds or Less |
| 5 | **5.1 – Being Persuasive In An Academic Presentation** – Substance Over Style |
| 6 | **6.1 – Presenting Progress** – Two Approaches |
| | **6.2 – Using Presentation Software** – Helping the Audience Follow Your Message |
| 7 | **7.1 – Problem/Solution Presentations** – Cause and Effect |
| 8 | **8.1 – Presenting Data** – Statistics, Tables and Graphs |
| | **8.2 – Research Presentations** – Finding and Filling A Gap |

In the Student's Book, **Learning Presentations** are introduced like this:

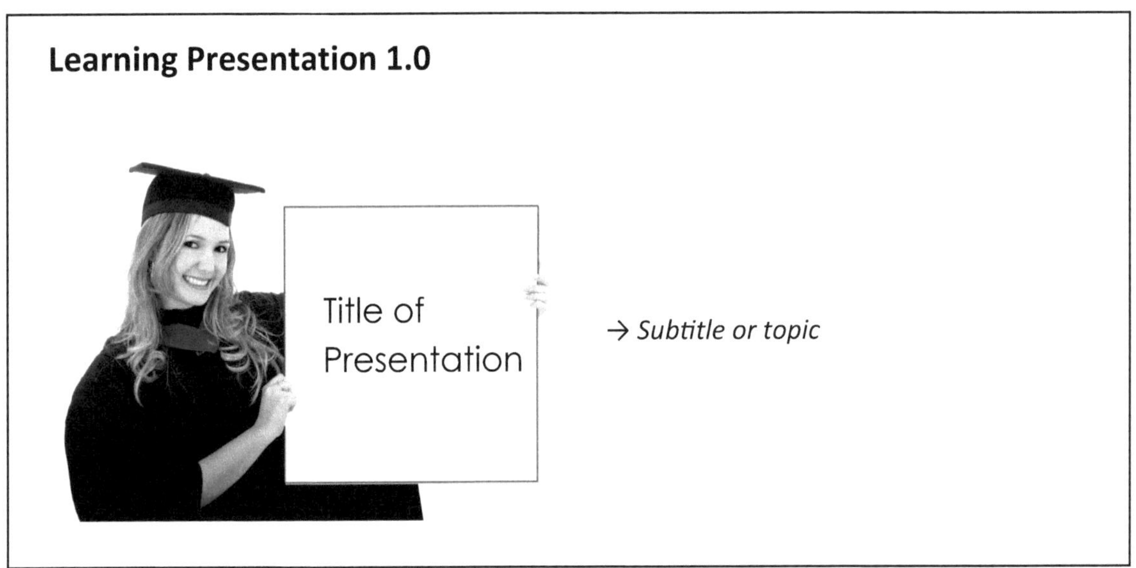



And **Sample Presentations** are identified like this:

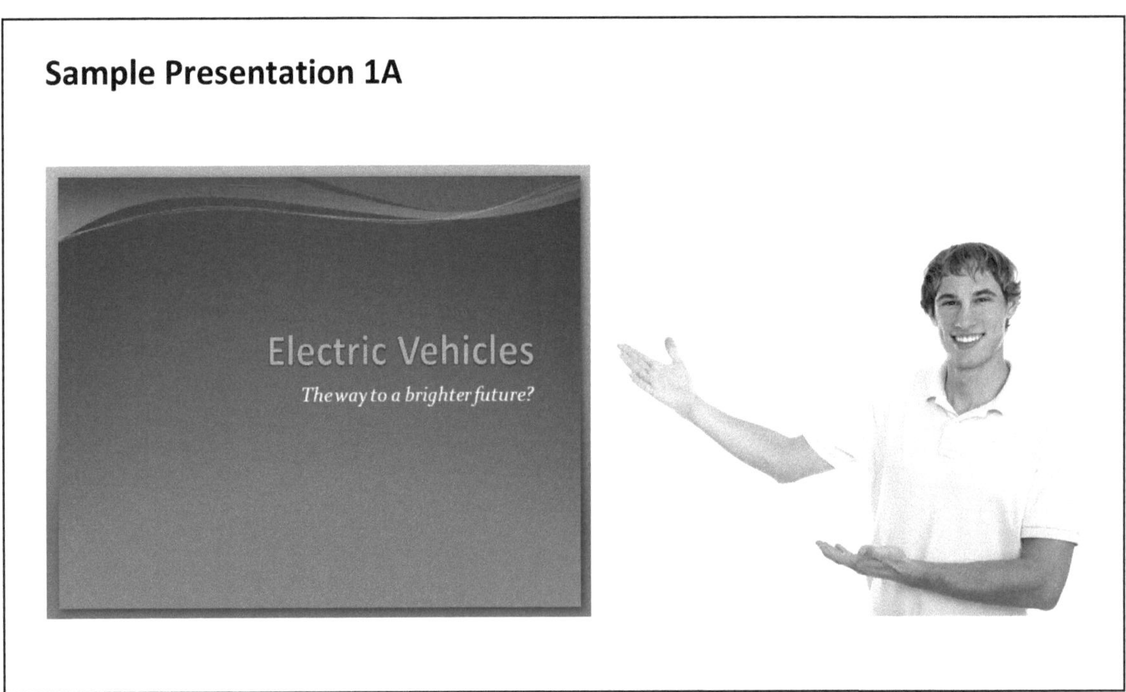

Due to the length, this video could be broken into sections and discussion could take place between sections (e.g. why is the audience important, how can nerves be controlled etc.). You could have the students review the whole video for homework. However, it is also good for students to see an extended presentation, as they may have to give lengthy presentations themselves.

## Signposting language

Signposting language is important in presentations. You might want to replay certain sections of the video so students can recognise how the presenter moves between sections. Suggest students have a presentation vocabulary book where they can make notes of useful expressions.

However, it is important to remind students that they are not game show hosts. Since the content of an academic presentation is what matters and time may be limited, such language needs to be kept to a minimum. For example, at the start of Presentation 1.1 there is quite a lengthy overview of the structure of the presentation. While this may be appropriate for a longer presentation, it would be a waste of valuable time in a short (10 minute) presentation.

## A good presentation

At this point, the students are not thinking about academic presentations but presentations in general. Brainstorming ideas in small groups or whole class should generate ideas for dos and don'ts of presenting. Encourage students to make notes which they may return to and edit as they watch the upcoming Learning Presentation.

Before watching the Learning Presentation you might ask a couple of students to give a very short (1 minute) presentation about what they or their group thinks makes a good presentation. Getting students to present without visual aids is an important step in developing their presentation skills so they will come to see visual aids as a support for a presentation which, while very useful, may not always be necessary.

# Unit 2
# What is an Academic Presentation?

This unit considers the particular features which make a presentation academic. Essentially this means highlighting the issue of *intertextuality* with students and emphasising that an academic presentation fits into a wider debate and has to be supported by sources.

**Aims & Objectives**
To raise students' awareness of key features of academic presentations
- provide an overview of the defining features of academic presentations
- focus students on the technical aspects of presenting (use of body language and voice)

The initial discussion on the features and types of academic presentation may not take long, depending on how much students are aware of already. To help inform their discussion you could show the three Sample Presentations before asking them to try to come up with ideas of the defining characteristics of an academic presentation.

**SP 2A, 2B & 2C**
A brief analysis of the Sample Presentations is provided at the back of the Student's Book. Before looking at the analysis, watch each presentation and encourage students to discuss whether it was

a) a good presentation
b) an academic presentation.

Once they have become confident delivering the text, encourage them to do so without looking at their books. This puts the emphasis back on the message rather than delivery. Make it clear you do not expect them to remember the text perfectly, but you do want them to present the main ideas of the text, and present them while using strategies to vary their voice to increase the impact of the presentation on the audience. This will be an important step to lead students away from relying on a script

read e.g. highlighting points they feel are most useful, writing questions about things they don't understand or want to know more about).

Since this is a presentation course there is no need to go into great depth about reading strategies or varieties of note-making, but it is important that students understand that they need to have a reaction to what they read. If that reaction is that the paper is difficult to read and not particularly useful, then that is fine. Within a seminar presentation they could talk about those issues.

**SP 3A & 3B**
Prior to watching these presentations, you could ask students to present the paper they have read to the group, particularly if you have divided the reading between students. However, it is important that students are familiar with *both* papers before watching these presentations.

**SP 3A** – this is a relatively poor presentation of a paper. While the presenter identifies the main points of the paper, there is no interpretation, reaction or evaluation. After watching this presentation, ask the students if they think it was a good presentation. Then ask if they learned anything new from the presentation they didn't learn from the paper.

**SP 3B** – This is a more successful presentation in that the presenter is selective with the information presented and, more importantly, has a clear reaction to the ideas in the paper and suggests what those ideas mean in their own context. Focus students' attention on the way the presentation is not a repetition of the paper's perspective, but is rather a clear expression of the presenter's perspective.

**LP 3.1 – Presenting A Paper**
Prior to watching this presentation, have the students brainstorm what makes a successful paper presentation, based on the sample video presentations they have watched and any presentations of the papers you may have asked the students to develop. While watching LP 3.1, have students add to these ideas if anything new comes up.

**Language Focus** – when discussing papers, students are going to have to make their reactions clear. This introduction to the language of stance will provide students with some different ways of expressing their opinion about a paper. With higher level students there could be an opportunity for brainstorming

# Project Introduction – Approaching a Topic

Over the course of *Academic Presenting and Presentations,* students are going to develop a presentation based on smart phones. This central topic was chosen as it is multi-disciplinary and could be approached from a wide range of academic fields.



During this project introduction, the main focus will be explaining the task to the students and starting to think of a focus for their presentations. The topic "brainstorming session" encourages students to approach a topic and consider it from different perspectives. One of the interesting things about this project presentation will be having students present on the same central topic (smartphones) but approach it from different viewpoints depending on their fields of interest or academic study. The introductory text is very heavily referenced to help inspire different ways of thinking about smartphones, serving as a launch pad for considering smartphones from different perspectives.

You could encourage your students to think of a question they want answered, since an academic presentation is often the answer to a question, e.g.

- Why are iPhones so popular?
- What do most people use their smartphone for?
- What are the dangers of using smartphones?
- How might smartphones develop in the future?

# Unit 4
# Elevator Pitch Poster Presentations

The elevator pitch is a style of presentation used in business to sell a concept quickly and efficiently. The general principles of an elevator pitch presentation can also be relevant to students in other disciplines as a way of focussing on the central message of their presentation and enabling them to present their ideas in a situation such as a trade fair or conference exhibition where they do not have long to engage the audience's attention.

**Aims & Objectives**
To raise students' awareness of the format and function of an elevator pitch poster presentation
- raise awareness of good design in visual aids
- provide strategies for dealing with group work and group presentations

While students may not be able to contribute much to the lead-in aims discussion about group work or elevator pitch presentations, based on the presentations they have seen so far as part of *Academic Presenting and Presentations*, they should have some ideas about what makes visual aids effective. Regarding the group work aspect, encourage students to consider if parts of a presentation should be separated so different members of the group work on different parts of the presentation or if there is another way to divide responsibilities.

## Working in groups

Before looking at the genre of the elevator pitch presentation, the unit opens with a discussion on group work. This is because the group presentation is common in

## Diplomatic language

Working in teams requires diplomacy and negotiation. Focus on some of the ways you can express disagreement in a positive and productive way.

## Poster presentations

In an elevator pitch presentation, posters are a common form of visual aid. Posters are also a good starting point for getting students to think about visual aids in depth as the general principles of good poster design are transferable to more sophisticated presentation software visual aids. As well as the posters in the book, see if you can get access to posters that have been produced by the students in the institution you work in. It would be particularly motivating for your students to see what their peers have produced and what is expected of posters in their courses.



## Presentation Task 4

This task is for students to produce an elevator pitch presentation on a topic they have some ideas about, based on the discussions and inputs so far in this unit. Tell the students that the 30-second time limit means that their presentation has

## Presentation Task 5

This presentation task brings together the different things discussed over the course of Unit 4. If your students do not have access to printing facilities which can produce A1 posters, A3 would be acceptable for the purpose of seeing how they design a poster. Alternatively, the poster could be designed as a PPT slide which students show.

Encourage students towards creativity and variety of approach to this task. The presentation could begin with the description of an event, or a list of great leaders, or a list of attributes necessary for leadership.

You could introduce an element of competition here and have the class vote on which they think (apart from their own) was the most successful presentation and why. Returning to the lesson aim questions would also be useful during the planning and preparation phase of this task.

**Presentation Task 6**

This is quite a superficial task in the sense that it is not expected that the students research and collect support for their arguments. It will be a purely opinion-driven presentation to give students experience of delivering a persuasive presentation. This will also give them a presentation that they can reconsider when thinking about what makes for a successful *academic* persuasive presentation.

Topics are not limited to the three suggested in the book; this could be an opportunity to localise the material and bring in a topic relevant to your students. Rather than letting students decide their position, you could give them positions to take, one pair presenting in favour of the topic, one pair presenting against the topic and the rest of the class determining which presentation was more persuasive. Avoid letting the class turn into a debate, but during the preparation phase ask students to consider the alternative viewpoint and how they could deal with the opposing view in the course of their presentation. This idea of argument and counter argument is an important feature of academic presentations.

## Research methods

In Unit 3 the concept of research was introduced. This unit builds on that by considering different types of research methodology. It is not expected that this will make students expert researchers, but rather make them aware of some of the issues involved in selecting a research methodology. Even if the only research they do is in class (be that interviews with fellow students or class surveys), it is important that they are aware of different ways of doing research and associated pros and cons of different methodologies. Read the text reproduced in this unit and discuss different research approaches. Students can draw on their own experience to help understand different research methods.

offer some basic introductory texts that discuss strengths and weaknesses of research methods. Alternatively, it would also be a good opportunity to let the students conduct their own library or online research to come up with their own sources. There should be animated questions after each presentation.

The feedback for this presentation should revolve around how well argued and well supported it was. For the first time in the course, the academic integrity of the presentation matters.

# Unit 6
# Presenting Progress

During an extended project, students m
presentation. This is an opportunity for peopl
them to get some valuable feedback on the di

**Aims & Objectives**
To enable students to
- provide strate
- encourage stu

Progress presenta

## Language focus

Presenting progress is going to require students to talk about what they have done, what they are currently doing and what they still have to do. This will require using a full range of tenses and the exercise on page 81 of the Student's Book is an awareness-raising activity on appropriate tense usage. The exercise sentences are also useful indicators of the kinds of things students might be doing in the process of conducting an extended project. Depending on the language level of your students, you may or may not choose to discuss the use of perfect past and future tenses.



## Dealing with questions

The aspect of questions is a very important area of presenting. Throughout *Academic Presenting and Presentations* students should have been asking questions after the in-class peer presentations. They also saw a presenter dealing with questions in Unit 5. This should give them some ideas of strategies for dealing with questions.

When discussing the strategies, it should be stressed that a presenter should try to deal with the questions they are asked to the best of their ability.

- Panic and repetition are not positive strategies and should be avoided.
- Asking for clarification can gain valuable thinking time and may also make the focus of the question clearer.
- Reflection can be useful but should be done sparingly – the question was asked as the questioner wants to know what the presenter thinks.
- Deflection may be a reasonable response if the question is well off topic, but it can also suggest a lack of wider knowledge so it better avoided.
- Admission is acceptable, although it can be avoided by preparing a presentation thoroughly.

# Project Review –
# Giving a Progress Presentation

**Practice Presentation**

Students should have been working on their smartphone presentations. This presentation will be a good opportunity to see what the focus of each presentation is and how well the students are progressing. At this stage they should have a clear focus or question that their final presentation is going to address and have done some of the background reading or research to begin to support their presentation (this research does not have to be especially robust or in-depth – class surveys or small scale interviews are fine).

It is also important for students to demonstrate a clear path and a realistic timeline of what they have left to do.

If their presentation is designed to answer a question, that question doesn't have to be fully answered in this presentation. Make sure the students are preparing a progress presentation explaining their project and where they are in it rather than a final presentation explaining their findings.

# Unit 7
# Problem/Solution Presentations

The problem/solution presentation has quite a lot of flexibility in terms of structure and shares a lot of similarities with recommendation presentations.



## What is plagiarism?

This text introduces students to the concept of plagiarism and gives some examples of what plagiarism may involve. The two texts reproduced in this unit are good illustrations of plagiarism and effective paraphrase. You could ask your students to develop an effective paraphrase for the last paragraph of the text to give them an opportunity to practice avoiding plagiarism.

**Citing and referencing**

While citing is something students should cover in an academic writing course, it is important that they have some awareness of the conventions of referencing. If the Anglia link doesn't work there are many other universities which host similar interactive referencing guides. Comparing the reference slides of SP 4A and SP 5A will be a good illustration of how referencing shouldn't and should be done. As a follow-up exercise you could get the students to reformat the reference list for SP 4A correctly.

**LP 7.1 – Problem/Solution**
Before watching this Learning Presentation get the students to analyse the structure of the Sample Presentation and ask them to consider any alternative ways the presentation could have been organised. Compare their ideas with the structures proposed in LP 7.1.

**Presentation Task 9**

To try to reinforce the concept of not scripting a presentation, the basis of this task is proposing solutions to the issue of scripted presentations. The four texts shown in this context should enable the students to either propose solutions to the causes or effects of scripting, or both. During feedback consider how well the students used and successfully paraphrased the information from the input sources. Alternatively, students could give a presentation on a problem of their choosing but their presentation would have to be supported so would require more research time.

# Unit 8
# Research Presentations

This is the final presentation genre covered in *Academic Presenting and Presentations*, bringing together many of the issues and skills mentioned earlier in the course.

**Aims & Objectives**

To highlight the steps students should take in a research presentation to place their work in a wider context

- analyse the structure of research presentations to determine what makes a research presentation successful
- provide language for talking about graphs and data

The unit opens with a reminder of what research is. Now would be a good time to ask students to discuss what research they are carrying out/have carried out for their extended smartphone presentation project.

**SP 8A**

This is a good model presentation, which is well organised and effectively describes the research project and findings to the audience. However, in the discussion following the video, particularly in light of the questions the audience ask, consider as a class if something else could have been added to the presentation to make it more effective. Emphasise the need to anticipate things the audience may not understand and address this in the body of the presentation, time permitting.

**Language Focus**

Describing data will be an important part of student presentations. The language areas highlighted are the language of statistics and also the language of change and trends. The data provided in this section would give your students the opportunity to practice both of these. With the first data describing sales, make sure students don't try to describe the data in detail. A good exercise would be to increasingly limit the time they have to talk about the graph (30 seconds – 20 seconds – 10 seconds) to force them to be selective and determine what the key point they want to take from the graph is.

You could also take this opportunity to get students to practice presenting any data they may have gathered as part of their project.

**LP 8.2 – Research Presentations**
Before watching this Learning Presentation, get students to identify the steps the presenter took in SP 8A. Once they have a preliminary idea of structure, play the Learning Presentation and discuss as a group why each step has to be taken.

# Project Presentation – Giving a Final Presentation

Congratulations. Your students are now at the end of *Academic Presenting and Presentations*. As the final capstone presentation they should deliver their smartphone presentations. The A POINT planning sheet is provided to remind them to think about the features that make a presentation effective, with the additional criteria of support added to ensure they think about the academic aspect of the presentation.

Of all the presentations so far, this should be the most formal in terms of presenter dress, audience questions and expectations of quality. It is not required that the students have completed any primary research for this presentation but they should certainly be drawing on sources they have read to develop their argument.

Rather than giving the audience any worksheets to complete as the presentation is being delivered, the evaluation of this presentation should be holistic – how effectively does the presenter engage the audience and deliver a clear support

# Worksheets

The worksheets in the Student's Book can be used with any presentation given during this course or with any academic presentation given outside the context of the course. Some of the worksheets are designed to be used during the preparation stage; others are intended for use by the audience as a means of giving peer-group feedback on a presentation. There is some overlap in the coverage of the sheets so that participants can consider various aspects from slightly different perspectives.

They can also serve as inspiration for independently developed feedback and evaluation forms.

There is no set schedule for the use of these sheets as different students may benefit from different types of feedback at various phases of presenting and practising or might want to focus on different aspects of presenting at different times.

It is important to remember that a successful presentation is a presentation where all the different aspects of presenting reinforce each other.

... king in an English-medium

... students face, whatever

... rly challenging for non-

... will need support to

... outlines the theoretical

... *Presentations*, a

... ation skills

... art of their

... esentation

... As well as

the course of the academic year 2011-12, there was opportunity to observe students delivering presentations for their lecturers and it was while watching Environmental Science research presentations that the particular challenges of an academic presentation became clear.

One of the first students approached the presentation in a time-honoured manner, outlining the topic and content in the introduction, presenting the information in the main body of the presentation, and summarizing the main points in the conclusion. The student had strong presentation skills, spoke confidently and clearly and, from an EAP tutor perspective, seemed to have dealt with the task well. When it came to question time, however, the substance of the presentation was seriously challenged by the student's lecturers, who highlighted the academic rigor expected from student presentations.

A later student, while not as linguistically competent or confident as the first, gave a presentation which was much more positively received by the lecturers. The student achieved this by approaching the structure of the presentation in a more sophisticated way. The presentation opened with a review of the current research and knowledge in the area, which led to identifying the gap in knowledge and outlining what the research project was designed to find out. The speaker then moved through the methodology of the chosen approach, presented the results and in the discussion and conclusion, returned to the research question and evaluated how successfully the research goal had been achieved. By transposing the structure of a written research assignment to an oral presentation, the student was able to deal with the assignment successfully and when it was time for questions from lecturers, the student was able to deal with the questions confidently and appropriately. Despite being at a linguistic disadvantage compared to the earlier presenter, this student was able to present *academically* more effectively by focusing on the purpose of the presentation and

Chinese, with a small percentage (less than 10%) of non-Chinese students. These international students may be UK students on a campus exchange programme or students from countries as varied as Russia, Nigeria and Brazil following their full degree programmes at UNNC. To help students adjust to the expectations of 'Western' university education UNNC requires NNES students to do a foundation year, called the Preliminary Year, which is delivered by CELE and which focuses on developing student academic and language skills. Once students pass the Preliminary Year and enter their degree level studies, ongoing support is offered through the ASC.

One of the avenues of support open to students through the ASC is an academic advising service, whereby students can meet with an academic advisor to discuss an assignment they are working on or get help with a study-related issue they may be struggling with. Through watching a range of student draft presentations from students across different years of the university, it became apparent that the presentation workshops ASC offered to students, while superficially useful for developing generic presentation skills, were lacking in helping students deal with the full range of academic presentation tasks they may be faced with. Most of the feedback given to students by the ASC academic advisors was related to the organization and structure of student presentations rather than language-related issues. This may seem at odds with Alexander's contention that it could be delivery issues that students struggle with most in presentations (2008: 145), but in the same way that a student might have linguistically sophisticated writing skills (in terms of grammatical control and lexical flexibility) yet still find it difficult to write an academically sound essay, so might a student have effective presentation skills (in terms of delivery) and yet fail to deliver an academically sound presentation. That is not to say delivery issues are not important but to emphasise that students need to know what the expectations of an academic presentation are in order to present effectively and appropriately. They need to know what features make a presentation academic and develop strategies for dealing with and structuring different genres of presentation. The success of a

central traits that makes a presentation academic, and yet across the three stand-alone EAP presentation titles it is seldom discussed in any depth. Particularly, when we consider the wealth of material dedicated to the development of student academic writing (with five dedicated academic writing titles published in the summer of 2012 alone: *Effective Academic Writing* series [OUP], *Progressive Skills* and *Reading & Writing 2012* [Garnet Publishing], *Four Point Reading & Writing Intro* [Michigan University Press] *Academic Writing Skills* [Cambridge]), the relative paucity of material aimed at academic oral presentations becomes clear.

Perhaps a contributing factor to the issues indicated in current EAP presentation materials is the fact that the area of academic oral presentations seems somewhat under-researched. It is difficult to find much discussion on what is expected of an academic presentation. Recognition of the challenges facing NNES when delivering academic presentations can be found in Zappa-Hollman (2007), which identifies different genres of presentation, gives a brief overview of steps taken in a presentation and also highlights the attributes which can contribute to a successful academic presentation. While Miles (n.d.) discusses academic presentations, reminding us that students taking a presentation course may have a motivation wider than learning presentation skills, the question of what makes a presentation academic is not addressed. Nor does Webster (2002) touch on this when outlining a Halliday-inspired genre approach to presentations. Formal speaking was clearly identified in Ferris' 1998 study as an area of concern amongst university students but, unfortunately, lacked insight as to which particular aspects of formal speech were of most concern. This indicates there isn't a wide body of research available for materials developers to drawn on.

**Designing Academic Presenting and Presentations**

These materials were developed in the context of UNNC. However, from the outset it was intended that the material be suitable for a more global audience and be suitable for use in a wide range of EAP contexts, by both developing

Entrance to an English-medium university education usually requires an IELTS score or equivalent proof of English proficiency at the IELTS 5.5 level or above, indicating that the students are communicatively competent. They will typically be 18-22 years old, educated and their studying in an English-medium context would suggest they also have an international outlook. As discussed in Soureshjani and Ghanbari (2012), any presentation course will have to address areas of presenting which students feel are most important, helping students develop the details of their presentations, as well as helping with delivery issues such as body language and voice quality. Zappa-Hollman's (2007) findings that students need support with delivering presentations extemporaneously and managing the question and discussion stage of the presentation process were also influential in the design of *Academic Presenting and Presentations.*

Determining the needs of the student more closely is more difficult as their cultural background is unknown, as are their previous language learning experiences and preferred learning styles. However, what we know of language learning generally has also been considered in these materials. *Academic Presenting and Presentations* is highly authentic in terms of task and content type (Rubdy, in Tomlinson, 2007) and the students also get multiple exposure to teaching points which takes in to account Pienemann's teachability theory (Pienmann in Macaro, 2003) and Nunan's contention that learning does not follow predictable steps (Nunan in Carter & Nunan, 2004). Space has also been left for the local users (teachers) to adapt and supplement the materials to suit the needs of their local students. It is anticipated that material input will take one third of the teaching time, with another third being preparation time and the final third presentation time. As such there will be ample scope for teachers to address particular needs of students, e.g. specific pronunciation issues, or lexical development.

Graves (2000) points out that aside from the needs of the intended learners, it is also important to investigate the needs of other stakeholders, the context in

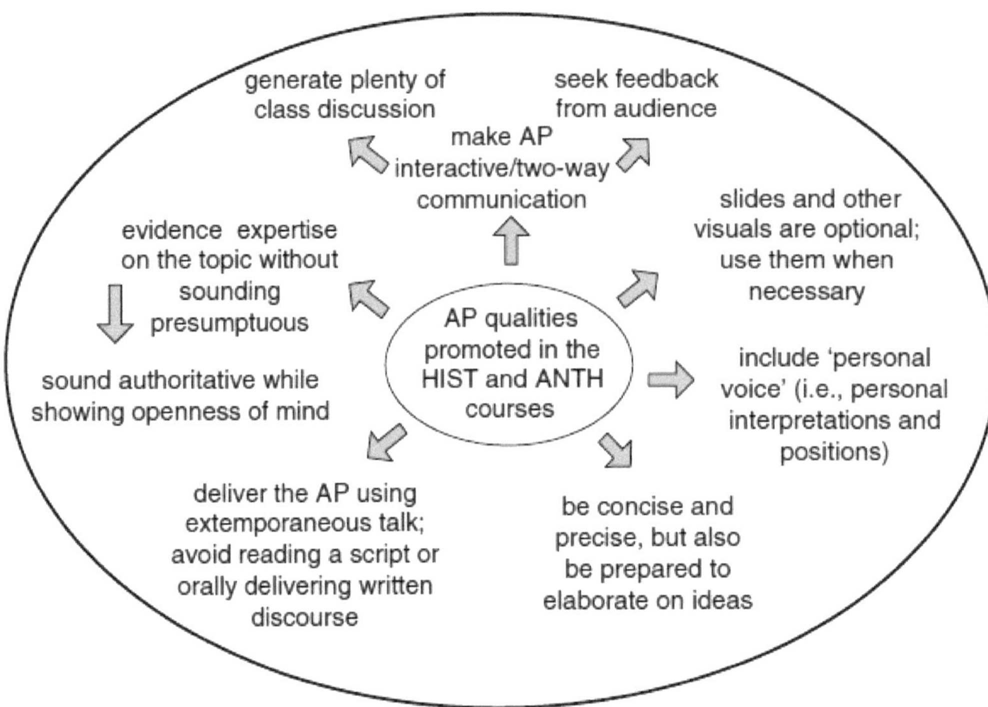


**Fig 1:** Positive Features of History or Anthropology Presentations (Zappa-Hollman, 2007) AP = Academic Presentations, HIST = History, ANTH = Anthropology

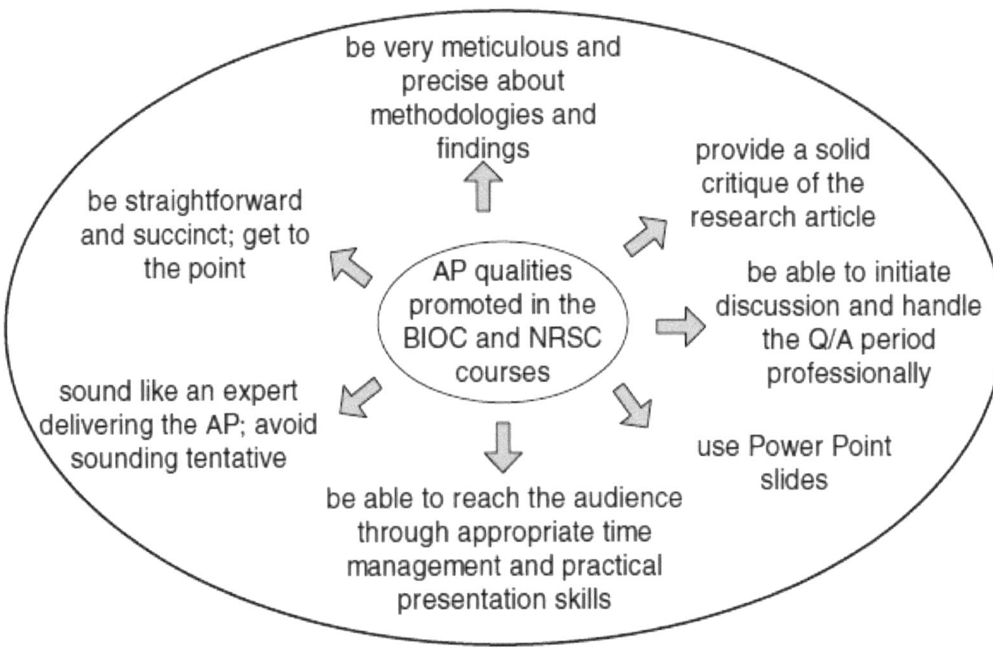


**Fig 2:** Positive Features of Biochemistry or Neuroscience Presentations (Zappa-Hollman 2007) AP = Academic Presentations, BIOC = Biochemistry, NRSC = Neuroscience

**Defining the scope of academic presentations**

As outlined at the start of this paper, there are many types of presentation task which university students may be asked to do, from formal assessments to informal seminar presentations. The thing that unites them, however, is that they take place in the university sphere and it could be argued that there are common expectations that cut across different academic disciplines. The interviews in Bolster (2012) and Zappa-Hollman (2007) made clear the rigorous standards lecturers have when it comes to presentations and that they are viewed in a similar light to academic essays. Indeed, it seems that while the medium may differ (oral and written) the key features of academic discourse are similar, with a clear parallel in the expectations of a good written assignment and a successful oral presentation. Issues such as overall structure, logical progression and firmly rooted conclusions based on reliable and verifiable evidence are as much a factor in oral presentations as in essays (Bolster, 2012). Oral presentations are also very much seen as a communicative act and the ability to make complex arguments or issues accessible to a wider public is highly valued (Bolster, 2012). A particular challenge of an oral presentation, however, is that students are expected to be able to articulate a knowledge outside of the content of the presentation. Where an academic essay represents the student's complete answer, in an oral presentation the student's ideas and arguments are open to questioning and it was widely felt by the lecturers that the question and answer stage of the presentation was the most valuable and insightful (Bolster, 2012). Essentially, an academic oral presentation contributes to, or promotes, further discussion (Bolster, 2012, Zappa-Hollman, 2007).

The scope and coverage of *Academic Presenting and Presentations* is therefore based on the following understanding of academic presentations, drawing together experience of working in the ASC and ideas from the papers outlined previously.

design and functionality of the material had been established. This was based on the following overarching principles, developed through experience of student presentations and influenced by the literature outlined above.

- There is no 'right' way to present, so observing and analysing multiple Sample Presentations will enable students to identify positive (and negative) presentation features; the course contains eleven different Sample Presentations across different genres of academic presentation.
- Students need ample opportunities to present in order to overcome nerves or fear of presenting and develop their own presentation style; there are eleven main presentation tasks in *Academic Presenting and Presentations*.
- Students have to develop competency in delivering different genres of academic presentation; there are six genres of academic presentation covered in the course.
- A successful academic presentation is about more than demonstrating good presentation technique; the presentation must be academically sound (see Unit 2).
- All of the presentation tasks the students are asked to do should fully reflect the type of presentations they may face in their academic studies.
- Academic presentations are time-bound, so there can be low tolerance for over-complex signposting language or padding.
- An academic presentation should avoid overt presentation gimmicks, but be engaging to motivate listening and later discussion (see Unit 5).
- Academic presentations must be supported by factual information; personal opinion alone is not adequate (see Unit 7).

When it comes to that overall design the intention was to develop materials that were theoretically sound and also practitioner friendly. The work of Tomlinson (in Tomlinson 2007) outlining guiding principles for materials was invaluable and ensured the emphasis was on producing material which was accessible, interactive, engaging, and needs-driven, qualities also valued by Dat (in Tomlinson 2007) when discussing the materials designed for the development of speaking skills.

## Course methodology

The importance of the methodology of materials cannot be overstated, especially as we are arguably in a time of "text-book defined practice" (Akbari, 2008 p. 647).

the most complex (Unit 8 - presenting a (research) project). In this way, each genre can be considered and its key features and steps highlighted - how a persuasive presentation may begin is very different to how a research presentation should begin, for example (see Units 5 and 8). This means going deeper into the structure of a presentation than simply introduction-body-conclusion, although the course avoids the temptation of being overly prescriptive. Within a single presentation there may be problem/solution, informative and persuasive elements so students will be encouraged to structure their presentations based on the objective of their presentation and the audience. For instance, when presenting a paper in a seminar, there are expectations of things students should do (e.g. adding a layer of evaluation and interpretation over simple reporting) that need to be highlighted to ensure successful completion of the task.

**Content-based instruction (Richards & Rogers, 2006)**

Topic selection for Academic *Presenting and Presentations* was carefully considered and although the course does not adopt a full Content and Language Integrated Learning (CLIL) approach as outlined in Coyle, Hood & Marsh (2010) in terms of being completely content-driven and aiming to encourage cognitive flexibility, it does borrow from the idea that content should be relevant and beneficial to learners in its own right, regardless of its later exploitation for language or presentation skill development. The initial plan was to have material that revolved around renewable energies, as this is both topical and potentially multi-disciplinary. However, as the course developed it was recognised that an extra layer of benefit could be added by changing the topic focus. Rather than, for example, students looking at a problem/solution presentation about new energy sources for a city, more could perhaps be gained by changing the topic to the problem/solution of plagiarism in academic work (see Unit 7). This approach would mean both students' presenting skills and wider academic skills and knowledge could be developed simultaneously. As an illustration of how this works in practice, in the unit on presenting a paper (Unit 3) the papers students

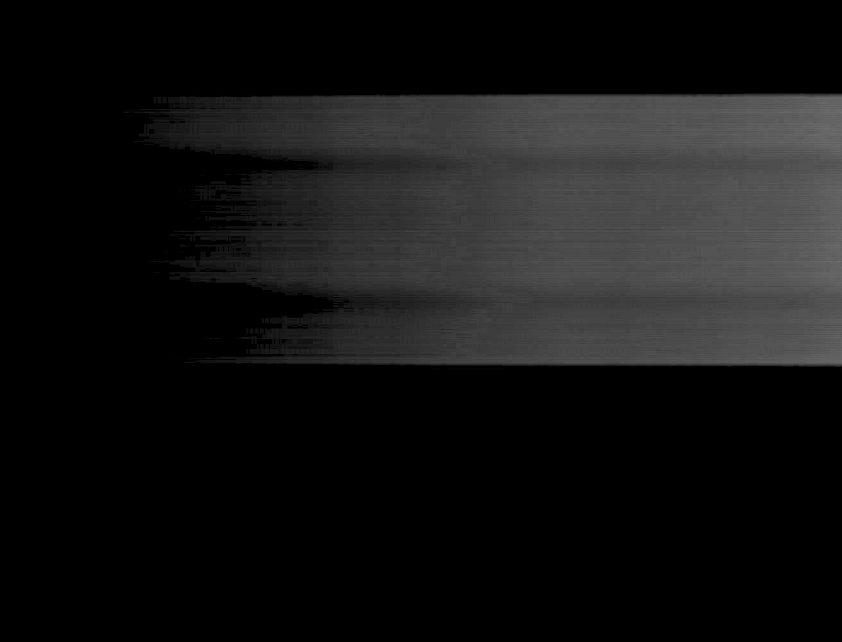

The eleven Sample Presentations illustrate various types of presentation to the students and the emphasis while watching these presentations will be on seeing how different presentations work and how a presentation can be delivered successfully.

The sixteen Learning Presentations take on more of a teaching role, giving students information and advice about different aspects of presenting.

**Course components**

The main components of *Academic Presenting and Presentations* are the Student's Book, the accompanying video material (Sample Presentations and Learning Presentations), the worksheets included at the back of the Student's Book and this Teacher's Book. The Student's Book is arranged linearly, with the expectation that students progress through the units in sequence. The material in the Student's Book is supplemented by additional/alternative activities set out in this Teacher's Book. This enables the class teacher to vary and expand the focus of the course according to student needs.

**A Flexible Course**

*Academic Presenting and Presentations* is designed for flexible delivery. Students will be given a directing focus when watching presentations in the Student's Book but the worksheets in the Student's Book can also be used to encourage students to focus on particular aspects of the presentations, e.g. academic integrity, structure, delivery or body language etc. These sheets can be used both with the presentations provided in the course and to guide peer feedback of in-class student presentations. This allows the classroom teacher to direct activities towards the needs of their students and could result in different students watching the same presentation and yet looking at different features.

As well as the presentations students have to produce throughout the course, there is also an extended project which leads to the students' final presentation. This project is an opportunity for students to apply the learning from *Academic*

# Comparison of Material Evaluation Results: Overview

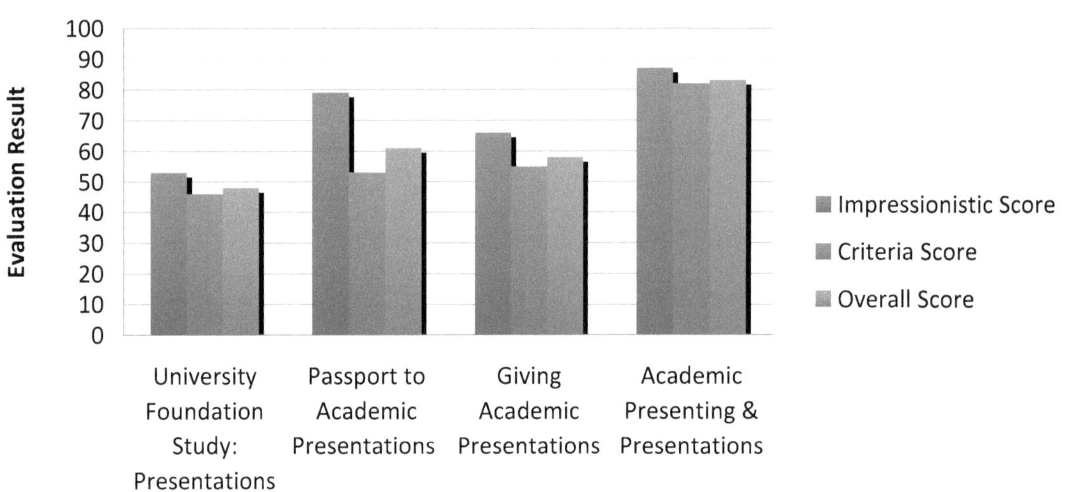



**Table 1:** *Overview of Evaluation Results*

# Comparison of Material Evaluation Results: By Criteria Categories

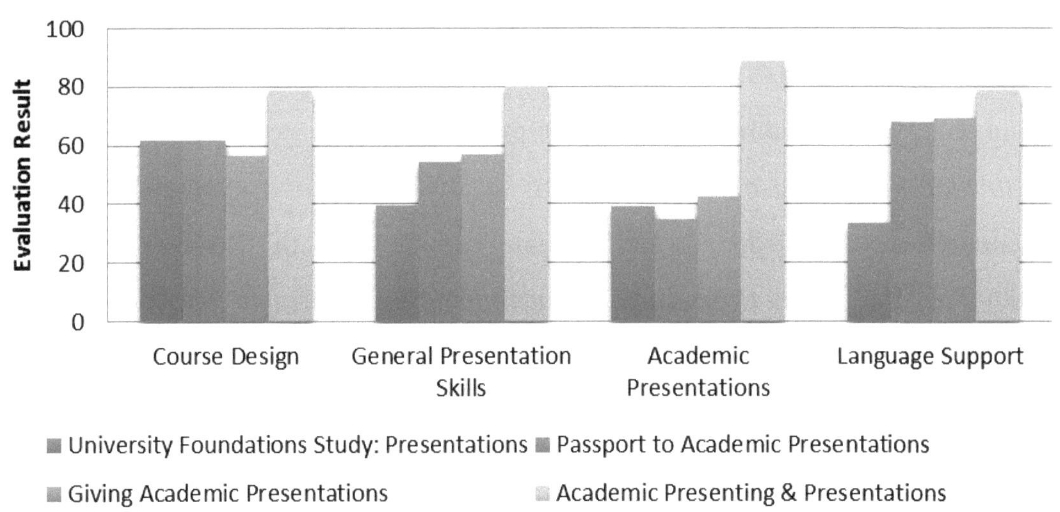



**Table 2:** *Comparison of Evaluation Results by Criteria Category*

# Bibliography


Akbari, R (2008) Postmethod Discourse and Practice. *TESOL Quarterly* Volume 42, Issue 4, pp. 641-652

Alexander, O, Argent, S & Spencer, J (2008) *EAP Essentials: A Teacher's Guide To Principles & Practice.* Reading: Garnet Publishing Ltd.

Barnard, R & Zemach, D (2007) Materials for Specific Purposes. In B. Tomlinson, ed. *Developing Materials for Language Teaching.* London: Continuum

Bell, D (2008) *Passport to Academic Presentations.* Reading: Garnet Education.

Bolster, A (2012) *Materials Evaluation Survey of EAP Presentation Materials.* MA Dissertation. Leeds Metropolitan University

Coyle, D, Hood P & Marsh, D (2010) *Content and Language Intgrated Learning.* Cambridge: Cambridge University Press.

Dat, B (2007) Materials For Developing Speaking Skills. In B. Tomlinson, ed. *Developing Materials for Language Teaching.* London: Continuum

Evans, S & Morrison B 'The first term at university: implications for EAP'. *ELT J* (2010) first published online November 25, 2010 doi:10.1093/elt/ccq072

Ferris, D (1998) Students' Views of Academic Aural/Oral Skills: A Comparative Needs Analysis. *TESOL Quarterly* Vol 32, Issue 2, pp. 289-316)

Ferris, D & Tagg, T (1996) Academic oral communication needs for EAP learners: what subject-matter instructors actually require. *TESOL Quarterly*, Vol. 30, pp. 31–58

Graves, K (2000) *Designing Language Courses: A Guide for Teachers.* Boston, MA: Heinle & Heinle

Harwood, N (2005) What do we want EAP materials for? *Journal of English for Academic Purposes* Volume 4, Issue 2, pp. 149-161

Webster, F (2002) A Genre Approach To Oral Presentations. *The Internet TESL Journal.* Available at http://iteslj.org/Techniques/Webster-OralPresentations.html (accessed 9 September 2012)

Zappa-Hollman, S (2007) Academic Presentations across Post-secondary Contexts: The Discourse Socialization of Non-native English Speaker. *The Canadian Modern Language Review.* Vol 63, N. 4, pp.455-485

# DEVELOPING LEARNER AUTONOMY THROUGH TASKS

Theory, Research, Practice
*By Andrzej Cirocki*

ISBN 978-1911369011

This book discusses the issue of fostering learner autonomy in the language classroom. Much research has been conducted into the area of learner autonomy, yet little has been reported on how learner autonomy can be developed through pedagogical tasks. This book examines the cultivation of learner autonomy through four different approaches: the learner-related, the classrooom-related, the resource-related and the technolgy-related. These approaches advocate implementing pedagogical tasks to enable learners to take responsibility for their own learning and presents a model for designing such tasks.

The book combines classroom theory, research and practice, immersed in the philosophy of social constructivism. According to this position, knowledge and learning are socially constructed, which means they both constitute the context for and result from human social interaction.

*This is the book everyone in the field has been waiting for. It is the product of excellent classroom-based research. It is highly engaging, relevant, readable and above all practical in its handling of the issues. Deserves to become the must-have book for EFL/ESL teachers, linguists, teacher-trainers, TESOL students, educational researchers and applied linguists.*

Prof. John McRae, University of Nottingham, UK

*This book is a perfect combination of theoretical and practical proposals that make it possible to implement and foster learner autonomy in the EFL/ESL classroom. Providing a model of task design, the author convincingly argues that learner autonomy requires carefully constructed tasks, and teachers who are competent designers of classroom tasks and materials.*

Prof. Wolfgang Hallet, Justus Liebig University Giessen, Germany

## Teaching EFL Online

An e-moderator's report
*By Andrew R. Webster*

ISBN 978-3848209422

This study explores the role played by the e-moderator in creating and teaching an online course in English as a Foreign Language. It details relevant theories of online learning and shows how they are represented through various models, creating a framework to assist the e-moderation process.

## EFL Communication Strategies in Second Life

An exploratory study
*By Susan Gowans*

ISBN 978-3848216987

This book reports the findings of an exploratory case study examining the communication strategies used between a small group of adult EFL learners and their teacher during meaning-focused conversation tasks in the virtual 3D world of Second Life. Discourse analysis of the session transcript offers insights into areas of language such as power relations, politeness and risk taking strategies.

## The Fractal Approach to Teaching English as a Foreign Language

Dynamism and Change in ELT
*By Maurice Claypole*

ISBN 978-3839133828

The fractal approach envisages a new paradigm of language based on forms found in nature and indicates a goal-oriented method of developing teaching materials incorporating a holistic view of language acquisition.

## Controversies in ELT

What you always wanted to know about teaching English but were afraid to ask
*By Maurice Claypole*

ISBN 978-3839139172

A collection of controversial essays relating to English language teaching, including chapters on *The Death Of the Communicative Approach, Teaching the Language of Sex, Non-native User Teachers* and *Parapsychology in ELT*.

www.linguabooks.com